CONTENTS

ABOUT THE AUTHOR

A popular speaker, author, and blogger, **ERIN DAVIS** is passionately committed to sharing God's truth with others. She is the author of several books including *Graffiti: Learning to See the Art in Ourselves*, *True Princess: Embracing Humility in an All About Me World*, *Beyond Bath Time*, and the *One Girl Series*.

Erin lives on a small farm in the midwest with her husband and kids. When she's not writing, you can find her herding goats, chickens, and children.

INTRO

There's Just Something About A Story...

- ❖ Romeo and Juliet's fateful kiss.
- ❖ The race of the tortoise and the hare.
- ❖ Cinderella and the shoe that changed everything.

Stories inspire us. They entertain us. They make us laugh or cry (or both!). The best stories can be told over and over and still capture our hearts. But what makes a story great exactly? What's the difference between a tale that is forgettable and one that keeps us on the edge of our seats? I think it's the story behind the story, the deeper lesson that only a good story can teach.

Romeo and Juliet isn't just about two people in love; it's about the tendency of love to break all the rules. The tortoise and the hare would be dull if it was only about a track meet between a turtle and a rabbit. Instead, it teaches us the lesson that "slow and steady wins the race" and reminds us all to keep pressing toward the finish line. There are all kinds of hidden treasures in Cinderella's story. It highlights the idea that love wins and good triumphs in the end. It makes us pine for our own fairy godmother who can get us a date, ride, and fabulous outfit with the wave of a wand. And ultimately, it shows us that even average girls can catch the eye of Prince Charming.

A great story is simply the canvas upon which something beautiful is displayed. That's why this study is all about stories. Specifically, we'll look at the stories of women who personally encountered Jesus. Spoiler alert—in every story, lives were changed forever. I'm hoping this study has the same effect on you.

Some of these encounters may feel familiar to you, but like all great stories, we can revisit them over and over and learn something new each time. Other stories may be new to you—like breaking the binding on a brand new book. I promise, they will soon be among your favorites.

The encounters in this study are great stories for sure, but our focus will be on the one character present in every scene—Jesus. These stories will entertain, inspire, and challenge us. But ultimately, they're so much more than good stories; they're stories with the power to change us because of what they teach us about Jesus.

So brace yourself for the beautiful lessons and realities that come to life in the stories that follow. My prayer is that you'll have your own encounters with Jesus along the way.

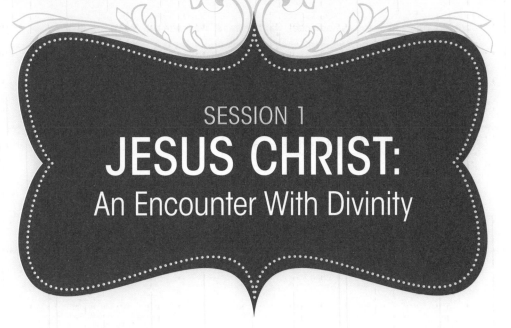

SESSION 1
JESUS CHRIST:
An Encounter With Divinity

WHAT IS DIVINITY? Divinity is a fancy word for the very nature of God. Not to be confused with the sticky, white candy your grandmother makes every Christmas.

Divinity is a big deal! It is what makes God, well...God! Wrapping our heads around this concept of divinity can be tricky, but recognizing the divine nature of God is essential to knowing Him.

What conclusion can you come to from the following equation:
If DIVINITY = GOD and DIVINITY = JESUS then _____ = _____

Why is the statement Jesus = God so significant? Let's look back at Jesus' life for the answer. At what exact moment did humanity recognize that Jesus was God? Was it...
- ❑ When He worked His first miracle?
- ❑ When He preached His first sermon?
- ❑ When the people of Jerusalem threw a parade in His honor?
- ❑ When He stood up to the religious leaders of His day?
- ❑ When He rose from the dead?

While all of these moments put Jesus' divinity on full display, the truth is they just confirmed what had been true from the very beginning. Before He had the chance to do or say anything in human form, His divine nature was evident to those anxiously awaiting the Messiah.

In this session, we will catch a glimpse of His glory through the eyes of two women. Their encounters will be the canvas upon which we will see a beautiful picture of God the Son.

Scripture refers to Jesus as Immanuel, which means "God with us." Write words or phrases that describe how you feel when you think about Jesus as Immanuel.

OVERJOYED: ELIZABETH'S STORY

Read Luke 1:5-25

Based on these verses how would you describe Elizabeth and Zechariah?

My husband, Zechariah, is a respected priest from a long line of priests. I am a descendant of Aaron who was the brother and right hand man of Moses himself. We knew the stories of God. We heard about the amazing things God had done, and we believed He was sending the Savior. We longed for His arrival. Even as we waited, there was something else that lingered in our minds. We had prayed many years for a child of our own. When my brown hair turned grey and lines appeared on my face, I stopped hoping for a child. Then God did the impossible! I marveled at what God had finally done in my womb but I soon discovered there was much more to celebrate! One day Mary, my sweet relative, burst into our house excitedly and before she could tell me her news, the baby in my womb began to dance inside me! And I just knew—Mary's baby was the Messiah, Immanuel.

Love, Elizabeth

Describe some of the emotions you think Elizabeth would have felt as she faced years of infertility.

Have you ever waited a long time for something to happen?

❖ **Describe in one word how you felt while you waited** _____.

❖ **Describe in one word how you felt when it finally happened** _____.

Glance back at verses 13-17. Make a list of everything the angel says Elizabeth's son, John, would do and be a part of in his lifetime.

Read Luke 1:39-45.

Elizabeth encountered Jesus' divinity even before she could see Him in the flesh. Her response and the response of the child in her own womb was joy.

Have you ever encountered Jesus in a way that left you overjoyed in His presence? Share about that experience.

OVERWHELMED: ANNA'S STORY

Read Luke 2:36-38.

When Jesus was still a baby, Mary and Joseph took Him to the temple in Jerusalem to dedicate Him and offer a sacrifice in obedience to God's law. While they were there, another life changing encounter occurred.

I was once a young bride in love. But only seven years after my wedding, my husband suddenly died, and I was left a widow. I suppose I could have married again, but I chose a different life. I've spent the past eight decades focused on my great God. In fact, I live in the temple and spend my days fasting and praying for God to send a Savior. I watch and wait for God to move. Then one day it happened. I'll never forget the first time I saw Him. He was wrapped up tightly in a blanket, held by His young mother. At first glance, He looked like any ordinary Jewish baby. He didn't wear a crown, nor did He have an entourage. There wasn't really anything miraculous about His appearance. But I knew that this seemingly ordinary baby was the Messiah I had spent my life waiting for. I was overwhelmed! After that day, I never stopped talking about my encounter with Immanuel. I told anyone and everyone the good news—the Savior had come!

Love, Anna

How did Anna respond to Jesus in that moment?

After years of waiting, Anna became the first woman to publicly proclaim Jesus as the Messiah. Write a short journal entry from her perspective about that day.

A BEAUTIFUL RESPONSE

The stories of Elizabeth and Anna have many similarities. The Bible tells us that Elizabeth was "well along in years." That's a kind way of saying Elizabeth was old. We don't know her exact age, but Scripture is clear that she is not a young woman. Anna would qualify for a senior citizen discount too. The Bible also calls Anna "well along in years."

Two incredible encounters; two women forever changed by those moments. One of them knew to worship Him while He was still in His mother's womb. The other understood that she was in the presence of God, even though He was just a baby.

What can we learn from their encounters with divinity?

Look up the following verses. Next to each, write the name(s) of Jesus revealed in the passage.
- ❖ Isaiah 9:6 =
- ❖ Revelation 19:16 =
- ❖ John 1:29 =

Mighty God, King of Kings, the Lamb of God...these are just a few descriptions of Jesus. In His encounters with Elizabeth and Anna, He didn't "do" anything extraordinary. Yet even as an unborn baby or tiny infant, His divine nature was revealed.

Jesus' divinity is not dependent on what He does at any given moment or even how we feel about Him. Regardless of the circumstances, Jesus is God.

Underline that last statement. Write a few sentences explaining why it is significant.

THINK ABOUT IT

When Elizabeth and Anna encountered Jesus it caused a reaction. Elizabeth's baby leapt in her womb, and she celebrated loudly at finding herself in the presence of God.

Anna raced over to Jesus' parents and excitedly announced that He was the Savior the world had been waiting for. Then she continued to share the good news with anyone who would listen.

Both women waited with expectation for God to move. Both knew enough about God to realize when they were in His presence. Both were changed forever by an encounter with Jesus!

Think about your own life. Have you encountered the life-changing love and grace of Immanuel?

Maybe you've heard about Him or even sensed His presence, but it caused no response or change in your life. If so, you've missed the powerful reality of His deity. Many people have discovered His story and even sought His truth but never submitted to Him as Lord and Savior. The fact that He is "God with us" changes everything for those who recognize and respond to His divinity.

Do you have a relationship with Jesus that enables you to recognize His truth when He speaks to your heart?

Is there room in your schedule for daily encounters with Jesus?

You were asked a question at the beginning of this session: What makes the statement Jesus = God so significant? After seeing His divine nature revealed in these stories, has your answer to that question changed or expanded from your initial thoughts? If so, rewrite your answer below:

✤DAY 1: JESUS = FULLY GOD AND FULLY MAN
Read John 1:1.

This passage is describing Jesus. It teaches us that:
- ✤ Jesus has existed since _____.
- ✤ Jesus is _____ God.
- ✤ Jesus is _____.

Read John 1:14. Just like John 1:1, this passage describes Jesus as "the Word," but it reveals a new side of Him—His humanity.
- ✤ Jesus became _____.
- ✤ He came to live _____.

This is a powerful set of truths. Jesus existed before the beginning of time, He lives in heaven with God the Father, and He is part of the Trinity as God the Son. And yet, He put on human skin and came to live among us. He never stopped being God. He didn't give up His divinity to be human. He was fully God and fully man at the same time.

Understanding this reality is difficult for our finite minds, yet believing it is absolutely essential to our faith in Him as Savior. As you consider these deep foundational truths, celebrate both the mystery and the beauty of His divinity.

Close today by thanking Jesus for being Immanuel: God with us!

✤DAY 2: BEEN THERE. DONE THAT.
In the verses below, circle the words/phrases that describe Jesus and underline any section that describes how we should respond to Him.

"Therefore, since we have a great high priest who has passed through the heavens—Jesus the Son of God—let us hold fast to the confession. For we do not have a high priest who is unable to sympathize with our weakness, but One who has been tested in every way as we are, yet without sin. Therefore let us approach the throne of grace with boldness, so that we may receive mercy and find grace to help us at the proper time." —Hebrews 4:14-16

What was the role of the high priest before Jesus arrived on earth?

The high priest had permission from God to enter into His presence and offer sacrifices on behalf of the people. He stood between a holy God and sinful people.

Jesus became our Great High Priest. He was made in human form and was tempted in every way, yet He remained perfect and blameless. Whatever we experience as human beings, Jesus has been there. He knows what we're going through. He stands in the presence of God the Father and intercedes on our behalf. Because of that, we can approach God's throne with boldness.

Does the fact that Jesus has had many of the same experiences you've had make Him more approachable to you? Explain.

Close by approaching the throne of grace with boldness. Thank Him for the mercy and grace He extends as our Savior and Great High Priest!

✛ DAY 3: WHAT'S THE BIG DEAL ABOUT DIVINITY?

We like Jesus' human side. It's fascinating to think about the fact that He ate, drank, slept, and experienced emotions just like we do. However, His humanity is not all we need to see about Jesus.

There are over seven billion people currently living on the planet. In many ways, our experiences are similar and have been shared by people since the beginning of time. But only one person in all of history was both fully God and fully man. This is why Elizabeth and Anna reacted so strongly to what seemed like an ordinary baby—He was God wrapped in human skin.

Jesus' divinity tends to excite us less than His humanity. But why?

Perhaps it's because it's over our heads. We simply can't relate. We are drawn to what we understand, and we can't understand what it means to be God. But in order for us to truly encounter Jesus, we must recognize His divinity.

As you wrap up today's study, ask Jesus to show you more about His divine nature.

For further study, here are some divine characteristics that belong to God alone:
1. Eternal: Psalm 90:1-2, Hebrews 1:10-12
2. All-knowing (omniscient): Psalm 139:1-6, 1 Corinthians 2:10
3. Unchanging: Psalm 102:25-27, James 1:17
4. Present everywhere (omnipresent): 2 Chronicles 2:6, Psalm 139:7-10
5. Limitless: Job 42:2, Luke 1:37

✤ DAY 4: JESUS AND YOU

Look back at Luke 1:39-45 and 2:36-38.

Can you relate to the stories of Elizabeth and Anna? Has there ever been a time when you were sure that you were in God's presence? Write about that encounter.

Elizabeth and Anna knew the truth. Jesus' divinity was not dependent on their feelings or circumstances. He has always been God and will always be God.

Do you have this same confidence that Jesus is God all the time or do you struggle to trust Him when you can't "feel Him"?

How do you respond when He doesn't show up in the way you want Him to?

The Bible says that Jesus is God. That's true no matter what. Choose to hold on to that truth by finishing the sentences below.

Jesus, I acknowledge that you are God even when I feel like...

Jesus, I know that you are God because...

Jesus, I will choose to believe that you are God even when...

Coming face to face with the truth that Jesus is God is a game changer. It might cause you to exclaim loudly like Elizabeth did, or talk about Jesus non-stop like Anna, but Jesus' divinity should always cause us to respond!

SESSION 2
JESUS FORGIVES:
An Encounter with Grace

SHAME. GUILT. EMBARRASSMENT. An overwhelming urge to hide.

Most of us have felt these dark, painful emotions as a result of sin. We know when we've blown it and missed the mark God set for us. Sometimes we even find ourselves trapped in a pattern of sin that leaves us feeling worthless, unforgivable, used up, tossed out, or broken.

Can you think of a time when your sin left you feeling ashamed?

This session focuses on a woman who knew the same kind of shame you've felt. She was so defined by her sin, it was all people saw when they looked at her.

Is there something in your own life that you feel defines who you are? Think of it this way:

"When people look at me, all they see is _____."

When people looked at the woman we will study, all they saw was her sin. Most Bibles place a subtitle at the beginning of her story, introducing her as "the adulterous woman." We don't even know her name, only her mistakes.

Think about some of the "big mistakes" you've made in your own life. What would you give to go back and undo those moments?

The heartbeat of this story is about much more than messing up. Yes, it's about a woman caught in sin, but that's not how the story ends. Her life was changed in an instant when she encountered the Savior. Her story teaches us about sin, condemnation, humiliation, and grace. Ultimately, her life is the canvas on which Jesus chose to paint a remarkable picture of forgiveness.

FORGIVEN: THE ADULTEROUS WOMAN'S STORY

Read John 8:2-6.

Answer the following true/false questions based on the verses:

T or F   The woman in this story was falsely accused of breaking the law.
T or F   The woman in this story deserved to have her sins ignored.
T or F   The religious leaders in this story made a big deal about nothing.

The answer to all of the above questions is false. The woman in this story did sin. Verse 4 tells us she was "caught in the act of committing adultery." There was no denying she was guilty, and according to the Jewish law, the punishment she deserved was to be stoned. The religious leaders weren't being unreasonable. While their hearts were out of whack, ultimately they were being true to the religious law of the day. She deserved punishment, but that's not what Jesus gave her.

Write about a time when you did something wrong, but did not receive the punishment you deserved.

Imagine these events as they unfolded that day:

"My heart was racing. My palms were sweaty. I looked for an escape, but there was none. I was trapped by my shame and accusers. They were right—I was an adulterous woman, and there was no denying that now. I had been caught with a man who was not my husband. I knew that the Law said a woman like me was to be stoned to death. I wondered if death would be easier than parading my shame in front of so many people. They pushed me until I was in the very center of a large crowd. I felt so exposed. They yelled, "Adulterous, Adulterous!" Didn't they know my name? I closed my eyes and waited for it to be over. I heard them talking about me using words like, "law," "stone," and "condemn."

Sincerely, The Adulterous Woman

Have you ever felt like a group of people had it out for you or wanted to attack you?

What emotions did you feel during that time?

With that moment in mind, what would you have said to the adulterous woman if you had been present that day?

Read John 8:7.

What was Jesus saying to the religious leaders with this statement? Rephrase His words:

Read John 8:8-11.

With one word, describe the way Jesus responded to the woman:

"I wondered which accuser would take the first shot at me? I braced my body for impact, but nothing happened. I kept my eyes tightly shut. My head down. Suddenly, I noticed it was quiet. I slowly opened my eyes. All my accusers were gone. Jesus was the only one left and He didn't seem angry. In fact, there was something strange in His eyes. It looked like compassion. He stood up and said to me, "Woman, where are they? Has no one condemned you? Neither do I condemn you. Go and do not sin any more."

Sincerely, The Adulterous Woman

What would you say to Jesus in that moment as the adulterous woman?

A BEAUTIFUL RESPONSE

The story of the adulterous woman could be ripped straight from a movie script. An illicit affair. An angry mob. A life hanging in the balance. But what makes this story different from anything you've ever seen on the big screen is Jesus' response. This adulterous woman deserved punishment and death, but she got forgiveness.

Read John 8:11 again.

Which of these statements best describes Jesus' response to the woman's sin?
❏ Jesus ignored the woman's sin and tried to be her friend.
❏ Jesus confronted the woman's sin but lovingly commanded her to stop sinning.
❏ Jesus exaggerated the woman's sin and used it to point out that He was perfect.

Jesus didn't ignore the woman's sin or act like she hadn't messed up. Nor did He exaggerate her sin or proclaim it unforgivable. He pointed it out and simply commanded her to stop. He was offering her a new life in every way possible.

THINK ABOUT IT

Think about the sin in your own life. When you consider confessing it to Jesus, what do you fear His response will be?

We may worry that God will be harsh with us when we sin, but the Bible gives us a picture of a perfect Judge who is both righteous and compassionate.

Look up the following verses. Write them in your own words below.

❖   Isaiah 55:6-7

❖   Psalm 86:5

❖   Psalm 103:8-12

The clear message of Scripture is that while God in His holiness cannot stand our sin, He has provided a way for grace to cover us and forgiveness to redefine us. This is the most incredible news we will ever hear...or share with others!

In the space below, write a letter to Jesus thanking Him for His kindness and forgiveness.

As we wrap up this session, imagine stepping back in history to the time of this story. Put yourself in the place of the adulterous woman. Replace her sin with an area where you know you fail to measure up to God's standards. Close your eyes for a moment. Imagine being caught in your sin and being humiliated by others because of it. Then imagine Jesus gently urging you to stop sinning while freely offering forgiveness. How would you respond to Him?

Now put yourself in the role of the accusers. How do you respond when those you know mess up? Do you point them to the grace of God or stand in judgment over them?

What changes do you need to make as a result of the truths we have looked at in this session?

✤ DAY 1: TURNING THE LAW ON IT'S HEAD

Review John 8:4-5 and 8:11. These verses contrast two different responses to sin. The religious leaders interpreted God's Law to mean they had the right to punish sin. Jesus turned that idea on its head. Write Jesus' exact words to the accusers in John 8:7.

Only Jesus is without sin. Because of His divinity, He was the only one in the crowd that day with the authority to condemn the woman and yet, He did not.

While the act of sin may differ, we all fall painfully short of God's perfect standard. Not sure this is true? Below is an abbreviated version of the Ten Commandments. Underline any you've broken. Circle any you've followed perfectly.

1. Do not have other gods besides Me.
2. Do not worship anything but God.
3. Do not misuse the name of the Lord your God.
4. Remember the Sabbath day. Keep it holy.
5. Honor your father and your mother.
6. Do not murder.
7. Do not commit adultery.
8. Do not steal.
9. Do not lie about your neighbor.
10. Do not want what others have.

No one can follow the Law perfectly, but this is just part of the equation for understanding God's response to our sin. Look at the Law as one piece of a puzzle. Inside the puzzle piece, write how trying to live up to God's standard makes you feel. We will talk more about this in Day 2's devotion.

✤ DAY 2: PUNISHMENT SHUFFLE

Look up Romans 6:23. This passage contrasts two very different realities.

The punishment for sin is _____.   But God's free gift is _____.

According to this verse, the punishment (or wages) for sin is death. Instead of death, Jesus offered the adulterous woman forgiveness. So did her sins go unpunished? Did He let her off the hook? For answers, we must wrestle with a big concept called *propitiation*, which means full payment.

Read the verses below. Circle the word *propitiation* **each time you see it.**

"For all have sinned and fall short of the glory of God. They are justified freely by His grace through the redemption that is in Christ Jesus. God presented Him as a propitiation through faith in His blood, to demonstrate His righteousness, because in His restraint God passed over the sins previously committed." —Romans 3:23-25

"Love consists in this: not that we loved God, but that He loved us and sent His son to be the propitiation for our sins." —1 John 4:10

Who do these verses say is the propitiation for our sins?

The penalty for sin is death, but Jesus willingly paid that price because we were powerless to pay it. That's not the same as ignoring our sin. Instead, the debt for sin is transferred from us to Jesus. He makes the payment; He is the payment.

Propitiation is another critical piece of the puzzle we need to understand God's response to sin. Write your response to Jesus' willingness to pay the price for your sin in the puzzle piece. We will continue to learn more about grace in Day 3.

✤ DAY 3: WALK AWAY

Think about a time when someone got very angry with you for messing up. How did they show their anger?

The religious leaders responded to the adulterous woman's sin by shaming her, publicly humiliating her, and gathering to punish her.

How do you think these tactics made the woman feel?

In contrast, Jesus responded with kindness. How do you think this made her feel?

According to Romans 2:4, God's kindness is intended to lead you to _____.

Choose the best definition for repentance from the list below. Repentance means:
❏ To say you're sorry.
❏ To ask for help.
❏ To turn away from your sin.

True repentance is much more than simply saying you're sorry. You must acknowledge your need for God and ask for His help, but repentance also requires a complete 180 degree turn from sin. Knowing Jesus paid the price for sin and offers forgiveness should stir in you a desire to continually turn away from sin.

Write sins you need to walk away from in the puzzle piece. Ask God to show you how to live in the freedom of His forgiveness.

✛ DAY 4: JESUS AND YOU

When people looked at the woman in this story, all they could see was her sin. It became her label. Think about the labels you wear. It might be a sin, relationship, something about your family, or even an area of success that defines you.

Read John 8:6-10.

The Bible doesn't tell us what Jesus was writing in the sand that day, but I like to think He was giving the woman new labels. Others may have only seen her sin, but He saw so much more.

Look up the following verses. Write out the new label each one gives you.
   ❖ Romans 8:16-17 = When God looks at me, He sees...
   ❖ Romans 9:25 = When God looks at me, He sees....
   ❖ 1 John 2:12 = When God looks at me, He sees...

Are there any labels you are holding on to? Is there something that you think defines you that is contrary to how God defines you in His Word? Take some time to talk to Jesus about those labels. Ask Him to help you see yourself as He sees you.

SESSION 3
JESUS BEFRIENDS:
An Encounter with True Friendship

A GOOD FRIEND CAN PROVIDE EVERYTHING from a shoulder to cry on to a companion for a fantastic Friday night. A bad friend can break our hearts, take our stuff, and make life pretty miserable.

This session is all about friendship. In fact, you'll be introduced to the perfect friend in the next few pages. Before we get there, I want you to imagine your perfect friend.

Use the prompts below to describe the characteristics of a perfect friend.
- ✤ A perfect friend always...

- ✤ A perfect friend never...

- ✤ A perfect friend likes to...

- ✤ A perfect friend helps me...

My profile of the perfect friend would include someone whose ideal Friday night involves a plate of sushi, a bowl of ice cream, and a chick flick. My perfect friend would always agree with me. She would give me unlimited access to her closet and chunky jewelry collection.

But do food preferences or wardrobe swaps really make the perfect friend? For the answer to that question, allow me to introduce you to two women who discovered a thing or two about friendship. First, there's Martha, a classic Type-A personality who likes to stay busy. She's likely to spend time with friends on the go, doing something like training for a half marathon or serving meals to the homeless.

Then, there's Martha's sister, Mary. Mary is more emotional and easy going than her sister. She might like to take her friends to an impromptu art class or spend the afternoon taking a long walk in no particular direction.

Martha and Mary are very different from each other, but they have one thing in common—a friend who loves them perfectly through thick and thin. Keep reading for the story of their encounters with true friendship.

GOING DEEP: MARTHA'S STORY
Read Luke 10:38-42.

How would you describe Martha based on these verses?

"Some people say I'm a perfectionist. I say I just want to put my best foot forward. I will admit I have a tendency to get caught up in the task at hand, causing me to miss more important things like enjoying friends and family. I couldn't wait to invite Jesus over when I heard He was going to be in town. I love when He comes to my house because it gives me a chance to serve Him. I know a warm meal and a clean place to rest isn't much, but I want to do something—anything—to show Him my love. When Jesus arrived that day, I had His favorite meal in the oven. There was still so much to do and I expected my sister, Mary, to help me set the table, pour the drinks, and serve the meal. But to my dismay, she just sat there. She didn't lift a finger to help me. I was angry that she just sat with Jesus while I worked my fingers to the bone. Finally, I decided to vent to Jesus. I'll admit that His reaction surprised me."

Always, Martha

Can you relate to Martha? Are you like her? Take this short quiz below to find out. Circle your answers:

1. An afternoon with nothing to do would make you feel...
   a. antsy   b. relaxed

2. When you think of school, you think of...
   a. your grades   b. your friends

3. You would describe your personality as...
   a. frazzled   b. chill

4. The first thing you think of when you wake up in the morning is usually...
   a. the items on your to-do list
   b. the people you want to spend time with

5. What really makes you feel successful?
   a. big achievements
   b. strong relationships

If you answered mostly a's, you're probably cut from the same cloth as Martha.
If you answered mostly b's, you're likely more like Mary (more on her soon).

Because Martha was so distracted, she tends to get a bad rap as a controlling, clueless, busybody. But that's not what Jesus saw when He looked at Martha.

Read Luke 10:40-42 again.

List ways Jesus models true friendship in this encounter.

You might have noticed that Jesus gently rebukes and teaches Martha. He doesn't just say what she wants to hear, but He pushes her toward a deeper truth. He genuinely cares and gets involved. He meets Martha where she is and steers her back on track when she gets off course.

Think about a time when a true friend lovingly and respectfully approached you about an area where you needed to change. Write about that encounter below.

SOAKING IT UP: MARY'S STORY

Circle the words that you think best describe Mary in this encounter:

focused   lazy   rude   wise   relational   gentle   quiet   intentional

careless   flaky   calm   serene   preoccupied   relaxed   boring   uncompetitive

> *Martha is good at everything. She can do whatever she sets her mind to and she can do it better than anyone else I know. I often wish I was more like her. When she told me Jesus was coming over, I wanted to help her make a great meal. But as soon as He arrived, I forgot everything I was doing. It's not that I didn't care about what was for supper; it's just that being around Jesus makes me want to drop everything. Every time I am with Him I learn so much, and I am challenged to live the life I was created for. I could sense the tension in the room on that particular day. I could see that my decision to sit with Jesus aggravated my sister, but Jesus said that spending time with Him was the one thing that could never be taken away from me. That's what I love about Jesus. He accepts me the way that I am. He loves me and challenges me to live with God's kingdom in mind. I've never known another friend like Him.*
>
> *Blessings, Mary*

What was the "right choice" Mary made?

How did Jesus affirm Mary in this encounter?

How does Jesus affirm and encourage you in your relationship with Him?

A BEAUTIFUL RESPONSE

Read John 11:1-45

List ways Jesus proves He is a true friend to Mary and Martha in this encounter?

What was Martha's response to her brother's death?

What was Mary's response to her brother's death?

As expected, Martha and Mary respond differently to Jesus in the face of grief. Martha runs out to meet Him, desperate to talk about what happened. Mary waits for Jesus to ask for her, and then falls at His feet in tears. Again, we see that Jesus meets both sisters where they are. He respects their different personalities and responds to their grief in unique but equally loving ways.

In your own relationship with Jesus are you...
❏ Like Martha: run to Him with your problems and freely talk to Him about life.
❏ Like Mary: wait for Him to speak to your heart then respond with your emotions.

When talking to Jesus do you feel...
❏ Totally free to be yourself.
❏ Like you need to act differently to impress Him.

Jesus' response to Lazarus' death shows us another characteristic of a true friend. When Martha and Mary faced tragedy, Jesus didn't try to comfort them from a distance. He didn't send a card. He moved toward their grief. He walked into the storm with them and felt the emotions they felt. The Bible tells us He cared about their pain and even wept with them.

THINK ABOUT IT

Think about your profile of the perfect friend from the beginning of this session. Finish these sentences again, but keep Jesus in mind as the perfect friend this time.
 ✤ A perfect friend always...

 ✤ A perfect friend never...

 ✤ A perfect friend likes to...

 ✤ A perfect friend helps me...

Look up John 15:15. According to this verse, Jesus calls you His _____.

Jesus wasn't just Martha and Mary's friend. He offers that same true friendship to you. Spend some time in prayer thanking Him for being a true friend and asking Him to teach you how to be a true friend to others.

✢ DAY 1 = JESUS IS NOT MY HOMEBOY

Several years ago, a t-shirt with the message "Jesus is my homeboy" was popular. It made for a quirky slogan, but is that what friendship with Jesus is really like?

Look up these verses and write out how Jesus demonstrates friendship.

   ✢ Hebrews 13:5b

   ✢ John 15:13

   ✢ 1 Peter 5:7

Clearly, Jesus is no ordinary friend. With these truths in mind, design a new t-shirt with a slogan that best represents the kind of friend Jesus is.

✢ DAY 2: CHECKING BOXES

Martha's flustered response to her sister sitting at Jesus' feet revealed a deeper heart issue. Martha was worried about checking items off her to-do list. She measured her relationship with Jesus by things she could do for Him.

Do you ever feel like you need to do certain things to have a good relationship with Jesus? Check any boxes below describing things you do out of duty instead of out of love:

❑ Go to church   ❑ Avoid "bad stuff"   ❑ Volunteer at church
❑ Read my Bible   ❑ Listen to Christian music   ❑ Go on mission trips

All the items on that list are good things, but when we obsess over tasks and duties, we can easily become motivated by religion rather than relationship.

Read Luke 10:41-42. Fill in the blanks based on the truth Jesus was teaching Martha:

Do not be _____ and _____ about _____ things.

Based on verse 42, how would you describe a relationship with Jesus?

Jesus commends Mary for choosing the "one thing" that "will not be taken away." Spending time in prayer, Bible study, and worship is how you can choose the "one thing" that will deepen your relationship with Jesus. Choose Him this week!

✢ DAY 3: BEING THE RIGHT FRIEND
Quiz: What kind of friend are you?

1. You and your best friend are out to lunch at a fun restaurant. Do you...
   a. Spend most of the time talking about what's going on in your world.
   b. Ask lots of questions to figure out what's new in her world.
   c. Spend equal time talking and listening.
   d. Try to get your friend to talk about the latest gossip going around.

2. You find out that you and your friend have a crush on the same guy. Do you...
   a. Get super competitive and start strategizing ways to get to him first.
   b. Tell your friend she can have him. There are plenty of fish in the sea.
   c. Talk to your friend about it and suggest you both turn your attention elsewhere.
   d. Ask your other friends who they think is a better match for this particular guy.

3. A friend gets a lot of attention for her super cute new haircut. How do you feel?
   a. Jealous.
   b. Ready to make an appointment for new haircut yourself.
   c. Happy for her.
   d. Ready to trash talk her new style to your other friends.

4. When a friend calls you upset, you...
   a. Start talking about your own problems.
   b. Run over to her house to make her feel better.
   c. Pray with her, encourage her, and try to make her laugh.
   d. Listen and be encouraging, while texting others about your friend's drama.

✤ **Mostly A's:** You approach friendship with a "what's in it for me" mentality.
✤ **Mostly B's:** You are a giver who goes above and beyond to show friends they are important to you. Sometimes you can end up being a doormat for others.
✤ **Mostly C's:** You love having friends but don't need them in order to feel happy or fulfilled. You'd rather have a few close friends than a bunch of acquaintances.
✤ **Mostly D's:** You have a tendency to create friend drama, and it seems like one of your friends is always mad at you.

Look up each verse and write out how to be a good friend beside each one.

Romans 12:15
✤ A good friend...

Proverbs 17:9
✤ A good friend...

Proverbs 17:17
✤ A good friend...

Take the good friend challenge! For one week, make an effort to worry less about finding the right friends and concentrate instead on being the kind of friend Jesus models for us in Scripture. Go out of your way to look for people who need a friend and strive to be kind, caring, and attentive.

✤ DAY 4: JESUS AND YOU

Go back and review Jesus' words to Martha in Luke 10:41.

Imagine Jesus is speaking to you. What things distract you from your relationship with Him?

Just like He did with Martha in Luke 10, we find Jesus lovingly teaching His followers how to prioritize their lives in Matthew 6.

Look up Matthew 6:33. Jesus gives us a simple formula for how to order our days and manage our time in this verse. Fill in the blank below.

I can make Jesus my priority by seeking Him _____.

Create a space where you can spend regular time with Jesus free from distraction. It can be a chair in a secluded place, a corner of your closet that is away from noise and distractions, or a spot on your back porch where you can pray and read your Bible with a view of God's creation.

Make a date to seek Jesus in that place as often as possible this week.

SESSION 4
JESUS SATISFIES:
An Encounter with Living Water

Match the needs on the left with the solution on the right.

Thirst	Medicine
Hunger	Water
Loneliness	Companionship
Exhaustion	Food
Sickness	Sleep

Each pair represents a specific need and a sure solution. In these situations, trying to find any other solution would ultimately leave you frustrated. If you try sleeping to satisfy your thirst, you will wake up still thirsty. The same principal applies to the rest of this list.

For some needs, the solution is easy to see, but often we find ourselves looking for satisfaction in all the wrong places. This session introduces you to a woman who knows all about searching for satisfaction. In her case, she tried to fill an emptiness through romantic relationships. She moved from guy to guy hoping someone could fill the deepest longings of her heart, but nothing ever filled her up for long.

As the story begins, we find the woman in the middle of a normal day, conducting business as usual. But then, an encounter with Jesus stops her in her tracks and turns her world upside down. It's a story that ultimately gives the answer to a big question we all need to ask: Where can I find fulfillment in this life?

SATISFIED: THE SAMARITAN WOMAN'S STORY

Read John 4:1-10.

Do you remember a time when you were really thirsty? Describe it below.

The Samaritan Woman was certainly thirsty, but she didn't realize what she was thirsting for. She dropped her bucket into a well to pull up water for her physical thirst. What she found that day satisfied an even deeper need.

> *I'm a Samaritan. Some people say that means I am "unclean." I certainly know what it's like to be treated like a dirty rag. Most Jews go out of their way to avoid me. Maybe that's why I was so surprised when this man named Jesus talked to me. I saw Him sitting there when I arrived at the well. He looked tired but I kept my eyes down and concentrated on my work. I came to this well every day for water. How could I have known on that day I would meet the One who could take away my thirst forever? When He asked me for a drink, I looked around to see if anyone was watching us. What would they say about Him talking to me? But, He didn't seem to care who was watching. He talked to me like He knew me. That was refreshing, but to be honest, His words didn't make much sense to me at first. I knew that the man at the well was talking to me about more than drinking water, but it was hard for me to grasp what He was trying to tell me. Living water? Never thirst again? How was this possible?*
>
> *With Love, The Samaritan Woman*

What do you think Jesus was talking about when He said He would give her "living water"?

The following passages provide clues. Read each one and answer the questions.

1. Based on John 7:37-39, who provides living water?

2. Revelation 22:17 tells those who are thirsty to take the living water as a _____.

Put the truths of those two passages together.

Living water = a _____ given by _____ to anyone who is _____.

I don't think Jesus was talking about physical thirst when He described living water. Let's pick up where we left off with the Samaritan woman to find out more.

Read John 4:10-15.

Imagine that you are in the place of the Samaritan woman. Jesus is explaining a deep, spiritual truth to you, but you are having a hard time grasping what He is saying. Fill in the dialogue below as if you were talking to Jesus.

❖ **JESUS: "If you knew the gift of God, and who is saying to you, 'Give me a drink,' you would ask Him, and He would give you living water."**

❖ **YOU:**

❖ **JESUS: "Everyone who drinks from this water will get thirsty again. But whoever drinks from the water that I will give him will never get thirsty again—ever! In fact, the water I will give him will become a well of water springing up within him for eternal life."**

❖ **YOU:**

Read John 4:16-26.

The man at the well was no ordinary Jew. His words were direct and convicting, yet His presence gave me a peace I'd never felt before. When He told me to go find my husband, I told Him half of the truth. I don't have a husband at the moment, but I have before—five in fact. I keep hoping the man I am living with now will propose, but it doesn't look promising. Maybe this relationship is doomed to fail like all the others. The man at the well knew all of that, even though we'd never met before. Then He told me that a time was coming when true worshipers would worship in Spirit and in truth. He was talking about the coming Messiah. I had been told about the Messiah since I was a little girl. I knew that someday He would come and help us understand the things of God. But I never expected that I would meet the Messiah face to face!

With Love, The Samaritan Woman

Have you ever encountered Christ at an unexpected time or in an unexpected way? Describe that situation.

The Samaritan woman joined Elizabeth and Anna (session one) in watching and waiting for the Messiah who would save people from their sins. In this encounter, that Messiah met her exactly where she was and it changed her life forever.

A BEAUTIFUL RESPONSE
Read John 4:28-30.

Why do you think the Samaritan woman went to tell others about her encounter with Jesus?

Before she met Jesus, the Samaritan woman had known a lifetime of pain and rejection. We don't know why her relationships ended, but Scripture makes it clear that she had experienced heartbreak many times. It is likely that she was looking for fulfillment in romantic relationships.

Have you ever made that same mistake?

Maybe romance is not the "well" you run to. Maybe you're more likely to look to your grades, your appearance, or the praise of others for a sense of fulfillment. No matter what you run to, the Bible is clear that only God can satisfy your deepest longings.

Look up these verses. Write out what they teach us about God's unique ability to satisfy.

❖ Philippians 4:19

❖ Psalm 107:9

❖ Psalm 145:16

Only God is able to satisfy your soul. The Samaritan woman discovered this truth the day she met Jesus at the well. Suddenly, she had the answer for the thirstiness she'd been trying to quench in other relationships. It was like solving a lifelong mystery and she wasn't about to keep the answer to herself. She wanted others to know that the Messiah had come and He alone was able to satisfy.

THINK ABOUT IT

The core truth this story teaches is that only Jesus satisfies our deepest longings.

Make a list of your deepest desires. I'm not talking about material things, like a new car or closet full of fabulous clothes, but rather the deepest desires of your heart. Things like significance, purpose, hope, or love. Once you've completed your list, ask God to show you how He alone can satisfy these longings.

✛ DAY 1: LEAKY WELLS

Read Jeremiah 2:13. This passage describes two contrasting images.

The first image is a picture God uses when describing Himself. Fill in the blanks below based on this verse.

God is a _____ of _____ water.

The verse goes on to give a picture of what happens when God's people put their hope in something other than Him. Fill in the blanks below based on this verse.

Abandoning God is like digging a _____ that cannot hold _____.

In this passage, God may not be describing a total abandonment of the faith. He is more likely talking about what happens when we put our hope in something other than Him. We can either run to Him and find that He provides ultimate satisfaction (living water), or we can look to other things/people to satisfy us and find it is like pouring water into a well that leaks.

Draw a picture that illustrates this truth in the space below.

✛ DAY 2: BOY CRAZY VS. GOD CRAZY

Many girls look to guys to meet the longing of their hearts. Whether you are seeking attention from many guys or putting all your hope in one guy to satisfy your need for love, attention, and a bright future, it will end in emptiness. If you are looking to guys to fulfill what only God can satisfy, it will be like pouring water into a cracked well.

The woman at the well might have continued to put her hope in men if she hadn't encountered a better alternative. In the same way, you may never break the cycle of boy craziness until you learn the beauty of becoming God crazy.

For each of the following areas, ask yourself if you are training your heart to be boy crazy or God crazy. Circle your answer.

❖ Are the movies and television shows I watch most often training me to be...
    Boy crazy or God crazy

❖ Are the friends I spend the most time with helping me to be...
    Boy crazy or God crazy

❖ Are the songs on my iPod leading to thoughts that are...
    Boy crazy or God crazy

❖ Does what I spend time thinking about lead to a heart that is...
    Boy crazy or God crazy

❖ Does the way I spend my time reveal that I am more...
    Boy crazy or God crazy

Instead of focusing on your feelings for a guy, choose to concentrate on your love for God. Take some time now to tell Him how much you love Him and thank Him for meeting the deepest desires of your heart.

❖ DAY 3: TELL YOUR STORY

What was the last thing that you felt compelled to share? It might have been a secret, exciting news, or something that made you feel anxious.

Go back and review John 4:28-30. After Jesus encountered the Samaritan woman at the well, her first response was to tell others.

Look up 1 Peter 3:15. This passage encourages us to always be ready to give an answer for our hope. Another way to think of it is to be ready to share our testimony (which is simply the story of what God has done in our lives). A testimony doesn't have to be polished or well rehearsed. It is simply a description of how encountering Jesus has changed your life.

Have you ever shared your testimony?

Use the prompts to help you think through your testimony.

✤ My life before Jesus looked like…

✤ My encounter with Jesus happened…

✤ Life after that encounter is…

✤ DAY 4: JESUS AND YOU

Make a list of the 5 worst break-up lines you've ever heard.

1.
2.
3.
4.
5.

No matter how you say it, breaking up is tough. It's especially hard when you're the one being dumped because it almost always leads to feelings of rejection. The Samaritan women knew what it was like to experience rejection. In addition to a string of broken romantic relationships, she was rejected by her neighbors and deemed unworthy to talk to.

Have you ever felt rejected? What was the circumstance?

We all experience rejection from time to time. When that happens, it is good to hold on to the truth that God will never change His mind about us or reject us.

Read the following verses and rewrite them as a promise from God.

✤ Psalm 27:10:

✤ Deuteronomy 31:8:

✤ Psalm 94:14:

JESUS HEALS:
An Encounter with Power

Which of these medical mysteries actually occurred? Circle your answers.

a. A case of the hiccups lasting more than two years.

b. A disorder that makes people's skin turn blue.

c. A syndrome that gives people the appearance of a werewolf due to excessive hair growth.

d. A condition that keeps people from feeling physical pain of any kind.

Answers:

All of the above. Imagine what life would be like if you had any of those issues. Strange medical conditions can make for a good laugh, but when our bodies don't work right, it's usually no laughing matter. When was the last time you were sick? I'm not talking about a runny nose. I mean "can't get out of bed, please pass the Tylenol, even school would be better than this" sick?

Describe the sickest you've ever been in the space below.

When our bodies don't function properly, even for one day, we can quickly feel discouraged, desperate, weak, and needy. That's exactly how the two ladies in this session felt. One was a medical mystery. Her condition stumped doctors for more than a decade. She likely spent everything she had on pills, creams, treatments, and procedures, yet she only got worse. The second was a pre-teen, maybe about the same age as you, and she was on death's door. If she didn't get help soon, there would be no hope.

But hope stepped in when both ladies encountered Jesus. His healing power changed their lives forever.

Have you seen God's healing power on display? Write about a time when the Lord healed you or someone you know.

DESPERATE: THE STORY OF JARIUS' DAUGHTER
Read Luke 8:40-42.

What do we know about Jarius based on these verses?

Why do you think Jarius went to Jesus for help?

Below is a list of some of Jesus' miracles. Match the reference with the miracle performed:

John 4:46-54	Cleansed a man of a serious skin disease
Matthew 8:16-17	Gave sight to a man born blind
Luke 5:12-14	Healed a deaf man
Mark 2:1-12	Drove out demons; healed all who were sick
John 9:1-12	Healed the son of a royal official
Mark 7:31-37	Healed a paralyzed man

We see in these passages more evidence of Jesus' power to heal. These are examples of why people like Jarius came to Jesus for help. Read Luke 8:49-56.

What do you think Jarius felt the moment he heard his daughter had died?

Have you ever received bad news that felt hopeless? What was your first reaction?

I don't remember much about that day but I remember this—everything hurt. All I could do was lie very still on my bed. I knew I was sick, but I didn't realize how sick I was. I could tell my parents were worried. I heard them whispering with the doctor and I knew my mama was crying. Then I heard my dad's strong voice. "The Teacher," he yelled. "The Teacher will help us." I had heard about the Teacher—everyone in my town had. His name was Jesus. Everyone was talking about His power to heal, but I never imaged He would come to my house to see me. "I'm going," my dad exclaimed and left in a hurry. Not long after he was gone, everything in my world went dark. The next thing I remember is hearing someone say, "Child, get up!" and I knew it was the voice of the Teacher. I obeyed. When I opened my eyes, my parents looked amazed and excited. The Teacher was there. When I looked in His eyes, I knew He had done what no one else could do— He had given me life!

Sincerely, Jarius' Daughter

Imagine you are the girl in the story. What would you have said to Jesus?

Think back to the beginning of Jarius' daughter's story. Jarius went to Jesus and begged for Him to heal his daughter. Jesus agreed, and they headed to Jarius' house at once, but they didn't make it very far.

Read Luke 8:42-48. Here was a woman who had suffered for over a decade!

Is there an issue or problem in your life that you've been dealing with for a long time? How does it make you feel when you can't find relief?

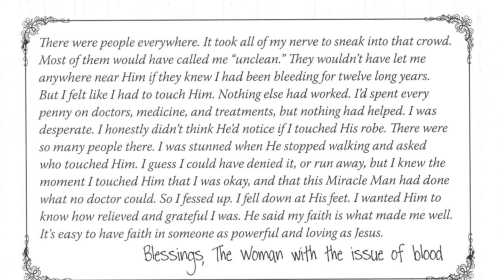

There were people everywhere. It took all of my nerve to sneak into that crowd. Most of them would have called me "unclean." They wouldn't have let me anywhere near Him if they knew I had been bleeding for twelve long years. But I felt like I had to touch Him. Nothing else had worked. I'd spent every penny on doctors, medicine, and treatments, but nothing had helped. I was desperate. I honestly didn't think He'd notice if I touched His robe. There were so many people there. I was stunned when He stopped walking and asked who touched Him. I guess I could have denied it, or run away, but I knew the moment I touched Him that I was okay, and that this Miracle Man had done what no doctor could. So I fessed up. I fell down at His feet. I wanted Him to know how relieved and grateful I was. He said my faith is what made me well. It's easy to have faith in someone as powerful and loving as Jesus.

Blessings, The woman with the issue of blood

Go back and read Luke 8:40-56 again. Using the chart below, write out the similarities between Jarius/Jarius' daughter and the woman with the issue of blood.

Jarius/Jarius' daughter   **Woman with the issue of blood**

A BEAUTIFUL RESPONSE

The lives of Jarius' daughter and the woman with the issue of blood collided when their desperation led them to Jesus. One was too weak to ask for help herself. She died from her sickness while Jesus was still on His way. And yet, even death was not beyond Jesus' healing touch. The other had been sick as long as Jarius' daughter had been alive. She had sought healing and found disappointment for over a decade until she had an encounter with the healing power of Jesus.

What can we learn from their stories?

Look up the verses below. Write what you see about God's healing power.
  ❖ **Psalm 41:3**

  ❖ **James 5:14-15**

  ❖ **Matthew 4:23**

The Bible is clear that God has the power to heal what is broken in our lives. Jesus demonstrated this power during His time on earth and the Bible promises that He has not changed since then (Heb. 13:8). He still has the supernatural   power to make the blind see, the lame walk, and the sick well.

THINK ABOUT IT

What do you need Jesus to heal in your own life? Finish the following sentences:
  ❖ **In my body I need Jesus to heal...**

  ❖ **In my heart I need Jesus to heal...**

  ❖ **In my relationships I need Jesus to heal...**

Both Jarius and the woman with the issue of blood came to Jesus in a state of desperation. He was their only hope. In the areas you listed above, are you desperate for Jesus to intervene or are you trying to "heal" what is broken in your own strength?

⚜ DAY 1: INTERRUPTED

Read Luke 8:26-41.

What had Jesus been doing before Jarius approached Him?

Review Luke 8:42-43.

What was Jesus doing when the woman with the issue of blood approached Him?

In both situations, Jesus was busy with something else when He was approached. When Jarius arrived, Jesus had just returned from a trip to heal a demon possessed man in a neighboring region. When He docked His boat, a crowd was waiting to hear the story of the miracle with their own ears. In the midst of the crowd was Jarius, desparate for Jesus' help. While on the way to heal Jarius' daughter, Jesus was interrupted again by the bleeding woman. To Jarius, the fact that Jesus stopped was probably frustrating. His daughter was on death's door and every second must have felt like an eternity. But Jesus stopped anyway. He dropped everything for both people in this story.

What was Jarius' occupation? (Luke 8:41)

What do we know about the bleeding woman's financial situation? (Luke 8:43)

Jarius was rich and powerful; the bleeding woman was poor and outcast. Yet, Jesus was willing to be interrupted to meet both of their needs.

Look up Ephesians 5:1. This verse calls us to be _____ of God.

Jesus paused to meet the needs of others, no matter their status. If we are going to be imitators of Christ, we must do the same.

Ask God to reveal the needs of several people in your sphere of influence. Make a list of those individuals and their needs. Next to each name, write one thing you can do to minister to them this week.

✣ DAY 2: WEIGHING YOUR WORTH

In addition to her medical problems, what other challenges do you think the woman with the issue of blood faced as a result of her illness?

She likely faced anxiety, depression, and hopelessness. Due to cultural norms, she was probably very isolated. People who knew about her condition would have considered her "unclean" and distanced themselves from her. The Bible tells us she also faced financial ruin. She spent every cent she had in an effort to get well.

What do you think all of this did to her feelings of self-worth?

Are there situations or issues in your own life that make you question your value?

What name did Jesus use to describe the bleeding woman in Luke 8:48?

Others may have only seen the woman's illness or poverty, but Jesus called her "daughter." He validated her worth, even in her most desperate moment. Jesus offers you the same validation.

What words does God use to describe you in these verses?
   ✣ Romans 9:25

   ✣ John 1:12

   ✣ John 15:15

✣ DAY 3: BEYOND THE MIRACLE

Fast forward from the day Jesus healed Jarius' daughter and the bleeding woman. What do you think their lives were like a year later? Five years later? Ten years later?

The truth is, both of these ladies went on to face challenges after their encounter with Jesus. They probably got sick again. Eventually, Jarius' daughter faced death a second time. The woman with the issue of blood may have faced another chronic condition. Eventually, she also died because of weakness in her body.

Since both women faced future sickness and eventual death, why do you think Jesus took the time to heal them that day?

Miracles get our attention, but physical healing is ultimately not God's most powerful work in our lives. The reason He displays His power by healing is to increase our faith in Him and show us just how big He is. The real purpose behind each miracle is to deepen our faith and glorify God in our circumstances.

Think about the areas of your life where you'd like to see Jesus work. Do you just want Him to make the problem go away or do you want His glory to be displayed in your circumstances? Explain.

✢ DAY 4: JESUS AND YOU

Read Luke 8:48 and fill in the blanks below.

"'Daughter,' He said to her, 'your _____ has made you _____.'"

Read Luke 8:50 and fill in the blanks below.

"Don't be _____. Only _____, and she will be made _____."

Look up Hebrews 11:1. Based on this verse, define faith.
Faith =

What do the following passages teach us about the importance of faith?
  ✦ Hebrews 11:6:

  ✦ Matthew 17:20:

  ✦ Matthew 13:58:

Clearly, Jarius' daughter could not heal herself. The woman with the issue of blood could not wish herself well. Only God could take away sickness and peel back death with a single touch or simple command! The people involved in these encounters did not have the power to heal, but they believed Jesus did. Jesus responds to genuine faith. Though He doesn't always manifest His power through physical healing, His divine touch can reach beyond our brokenness and heal us from the inside out.

Do you have faith that He can heal what is broken in your life?

SESSION 6
JESUS PURSUES:
An Encounter with Compassion

When was the last time you cried?

When was the last time you said to someone else, "don't cry"? What were the circumstances?

Sometimes when we tell others not to cry, we want them to stop the tears because it makes us uncomfortable. Other times, we simply don't know what else to say. But when Jesus says, "don't cry," He means something entirely different.

Review the story of Jarius' daughter (session five) in Luke 8:51-56. Why did Jesus tell the crowd to "stop crying"?

Jesus cut the mourners short because He was going to do something about their grief. To them, the situation seemed hopeless, but Jesus knew better. When He told them to stop crying, He wasn't asking them to suck it up and pretend that everything was okay. He was letting them know that hope was coming to a situation that seemed hopeless. He was moved with compassion for the girl and those who loved her.

If you were to define compassion in your own words, what would you say?

Who are the people in your life that you would describe as compassionate?

Compassion goes beyond feeling sorry for someone. Compassion = love in action.

In this session we will meet a woman who experienced Jesus' compassion first hand. She was facing an extraordinarily desperate situation. On her own, she could not pull herself out of the pit she was in. But Jesus' compassion changed everything.

Jesus did more than just express sympathy for the woman's situation. He was moved to action because her circumstances were grave. Her story shows us that Jesus is a compassionate God and reminds us of the importance of demonstrating compassion to those who are hurting around us.

HOPELESS: THE STORY OF THE WIDOW OF NAIN
Read Luke 7:11-12.

List the emotions the Widow of Nain likely experienced during this funeral.

No doubt this woman was grieved by the death of her son, but her situation was much more desperate than that. The Bible tells us she was a widow, meaning her husband had also died. In her culture, that would mean the responsibility to care for her financial and physical needs would shift to her son. Now, her only son was dead and she had been left absolutely destitute. To her and those who knew her, this woman's situation looked hopeless.

Have you ever faced a situation that looked absolutely hopeless? Write about it below.

Based on the following verses, where should we place our hope?
   ✧ Psalm 38:15

   ✧ Psalm 42:11

   ✧ Psalm 146:5

What does it mean to put your hope in God?

Read Luke 7:13-17.

Why did Jesus tell this grieving mother not to cry?

What would you think if you were a member of the crowd that day watching Jesus touch and talk to a dead body?

When I first saw Him, I thought He was just one of the mourners. He walked right up to me and said, "Don't cry." But how could I stop crying? My son was dead. Even so, I stopped. There was something different about Him. He moved quickly to my son's coffin and touched it. I couldn't believe what He was doing! Everyone knew touching a coffin that carried the dead made you ceremonially unclean. He didn't seem to notice or mind. Then He said, "Young man, I tell you, get up!" I held my breath. Suddenly I knew who this man was—It was Jesus. The stories of His power to heal were spreading like wildfire in our area. I knew that if anyone could bring my son back, He could. As soon as my son began to speak, Jesus brought him over to me. I held on as tightly as I could and didn't want to ever let go. What Jesus did for me that day was the most loving act I've ever experienced. He gave me back what I'd lost; He gave me hope. I will never forget His compassion.

Love, The Widow of Nain

Describe a time when someone showed you compassion by putting love into action.

A BEAUTIFUL RESPONSE

Go back and review Luke 7:16-17.

How did the crowd who witnessed this miracle respond?

The Bible records several responses to the resurrection of the widow's son.

1. Initial response = THEY EXPERIENCED FEAR

Why do you think they responded with fear?

The word *fear* in this passage may not mean that they were afraid. More likely, they developed a healthy sense of respect and awe because of the power Jesus demonstrated. The Bible calls us to have a similar response to God.

Look up Psalm 86:11 and rewrite it as a prayer below.

2. Next response = THEY GLORIFIED GOD

What two statements did the crowd make in Luke 7:16 that glorified God?

❖

❖

3. Final response = THEY TOLD OTHERS

I'm sure they told the story of the widow's son, but they didn't stop there. They instinctively knew that Jesus' ability to raise the dead made Him extraordinary. They proclaimed that Jesus was a great prophet and that God had visited them.

When Jesus puts love in action, He does more than just change our circumstances; He helps us to see Him for who He really is. An important takeaway from the widow's story is that compassion is a key aspect of Jesus' character. He sees our desperate circumstances and responds with love in action.

With that truth in mind, what advice can you give to a friend who feels like God does not care about her circumstances?

THINK ABOUT IT

The Bible records three accounts where Jesus raised someone else from the dead. We've looked at all of them in different sessions of this study. Here's a re-cap.

❖ Jesus raised Mary and Martha's brother, Lazarus from the dead (John 11:1-44).

❖ Jesus raised Jarius' daughter from the dead (Luke 8:40-56).

❖ Jesus raises the widow of Nain's son from the dead (Luke 7:11-17).

These are powerful stories that point to an even greater miracle...Jesus' authority over death. His victory over death is essential to our faith. We now serve a RISEN LORD (Matt. 28:1-10).

In this life, we will still have to bury those we love and death will remain an inevitable part of our experience. Our hope is set on Jesus whose compassion heals our brokenness and whose resurrection power gives us everlasting life.

In what ways have you experienced His compassion and resurrection power in your life?

✤ DAY 1: WIPE EVERY TEAR

Jesus was moved by the tears of the Widow of Nain. With compassion, He stepped into her moment of grief and spoke words of life into her situation.

What circumstances in your life make you feel sad?

What would you ask Jesus to change about your situation?

Psalm 56:8 gives a beautiful image of God's compassion in light of our tears. Read this verse then draw a picture of the image portrayed.

God sees our tears and is moved with compassion by our pain. Jesus could say to us, "don't cry," just like He said to the Widow of Nain—not because He wants us to pretend everything is okay, but because He has a plan to heal what is broken.

Look up these verses.
- ✤ **Isaiah 25:8**
- ✤ **Revelation 7:17**
- ✤ **Revelation 21:4**

God promises that one day He will wipe every _____ from every _____.

He may not change your circumstances today, but He sees your hurt and promises a day when you will cry no more.

How does that change your feelings about the circumstances you listed above?

✤ DAY 2: WHEN SOMETHING STAYS BURIED

The Widow of Nain's story had a happy ending—she got her son back. Jesus promises that a time is coming when He will wipe away our tears, but He does not promise to take away everything that causes pain right now. This can be an especially hard truth when we have to bury something, as in give it up forever. In fact, such sacrifices may make us feel hopeless at times.

What have you had to bury (literally or figuratively) in your lifetime?

How did you respond to that loss?

In what ways does the compassionate nature of Jesus help you deal with grief?

The Bible is clear that we will face difficult times in this life (John 16:33). We will have to bury things that God may never restore to us here on earth. But God assures us that even our pain can be used for good.

Look up Romans 8:28. Rewrite this verse in your own words.

You may be grieving the loss of a person, relationship, opportunity, or dream. Are you willing to let God heal your heart and help you move forward? If so, write out a prayer to God expressing your trust in Him no matter the outcome.

✢ DAY 3: PUT LOVE INTO ACTION

As a quick reminder, write the definition of compassion below (from page 48).

Think back over all of the encounters you've studied in this book. Make a list of practical ways Jesus demonstrated compassion to the individuals He met?

Read Ephesians 4:32.

Jesus demonstrated compassion and then called us to show compassion toward others. This calling is not always easy or convenient. Jesus went out of His way to find and help the truly desperate.

Make a list of 5 practical ways you can demonstrate love to others.
1.
2.
3.
4.
5.

Are you ready to put love into action? Take some time to ask Jesus to show you who needs to see love in action in your world. Follow His lead and seek to demonstrate compassion even when it is inconvenient or costly.

✤ DAY 4: JESUS AND YOU

Raising someone from the dead? That's impossible! At least it is for me and you. We don't have authority over death like Jesus does. In addition to seeing compassion in action, the widow's story reminds us that God is able to do the impossible.

Read Luke 1:37. This is another good reminder that nothing is impossible with God. He can raise the dead, heal the sick, and forgive our sins. He's a big God who can make big changes in us and accomplish great things through us. Even so, sometimes what He calls us to do can feel impossible. And that's okay. This reality should lead us to a deep dependence on God for everything we do.

Expressing compassion toward others can feel overwhelming or uncomfortable at times. Are there people in your life that you struggle to be compassionate toward? If so, why do you think that is?

It's natural to have reservations. Living with compassion will stretch you out of your comfort zone, but you don't have to do it alone. Jesus demonstrates compassion toward you and gives you the power to do the same for others.

End this time by praying specifically for the people you thought of earlier. Ask God to give you the courage and compassion you need to reach out to them.

SESSION 7
JESUS REIGNS:
An Encounter with Humility

List words or draw images that come to mind when you think about royalty.

Perhaps when you think of royalty, you imagine the fairy tale variety with a sprawling castle, huge throne, and great power. Maybe you imagine the modern royal family of Great Britain with their wedding spectaculars and headline grabbing antics. Either way, most of us think of power, authority, and celebrity status when we envision royalty.

Jesus has a way of turning our perspective upside down. Read Revelation 19:16. **This verse describes Jesus two ways:**

_____ of _____ and _____ of _____

Jesus is King all right. In fact, the Bible describes Him as the King of Kings and Lord of Lords. Power? Check. Riches? Check. Fame? Check! And yet, Jesus doesn't flaunt this while on earth. Instead, He demonstrates incredible humility.

Humility can be a difficult concept to grasp. Which of these definitions do you think best describes humility?
- ❏ Thinking poorly of yourself
- ❏ The state of being humble or not proud
- ❏ The opposite of expensive or luxurious
- ❏ Allowing others to treat you badly

Humility is hard for us to understand because we live in a culture that places great value on achievement, fame, and wealth. The people we consider to be the greatest tend to be the ones who have much, not the ones who serve much.

List people our society admires or holds in high esteem (past or present):
1.
2.
3.
4.
5.

Chances are you listed presidents, athletes, celebrities, or wealthy business gurus.
It's easy to admire those who seem to have it all, but what do you think is God's definition of greatness?

Jesus is our perfect example of greatness. Think back over what you've learned about Jesus in this study. In what ways have you seen Him demonstrate humility through the encounters you've studied in Scripture?

In the stories of...   Jesus demonstrated humility by...
❖ Elizabeth and Anna
❖ The Adulterous Woman
❖ Mary and Martha
❖ The Woman at the Well
❖ Jaruis' daughter/bleeding woman
❖ The Widow of Nain

Every step of the way, in every single encounter, Jesus responded to people with grace and humility. He did not demand worship or flaunt His divinity. He wasn't concerned with gaining wealth and power. Instead, He humbly served others.

In this session, we will witness an encounter between Jesus and a woman named Salome, the mother of James and John. In a brief conversation, Jesus redefines greatness and teaches us all a lesson about the beauty of living with humility.

REALITY CHECK: SALOME'S STORY

Read Matthew 20:20-23.

The woman in this story is Salome. She was the mother of James and John, two of the first men that Jesus called to be among His twelve disciples. They had seen Jesus perform miracles and heard Him preach on the kingdom of God. They believed that Jesus would one day rule the earth as King.

When Salome asked Jesus to let her sons sit on His right and left, what was she really asking of Him?

Salome's request was for her sons to have power, prestige, and authority. She was not the first to ask such a question. Look up Luke 9:46-48.

What were the disciples arguing about in these verses?

The disciples fought among themselves over who would be the greatest. Salome took matters into her own hands and asked Jesus to give her sons positions of honor in His kingdom. Jesus turned everyone's concept of greatness upside down.

I just wanted the best for my sons. I knew that Jesus was God in the flesh. I had seen Him work so many miracles and heard incredible stories about Him from James and John. My boys left everything—including our family fishing business—to follow Him. At first I was skeptical, but it didn't take long for me to realize Jesus was the King we had been waiting for. I knew some day He would rule over our land. I wanted my sons to be right there with Him when He did. I asked Jesus to let one sit on His right and the other on His left in His kingdom. I wasn't prepared for His answer. In fact, His response perplexed me. He seemed to be talking in riddles, but we all had a very different perspective of greatness by the end of that encounter.

With Love, Salome

What was Jesus referring to when He mentioned "the cup" he was about to drink?

Read Matthew 26:36-39.

James and John soon discovered "the cup" Jesus mentioned. He was referring to His coming death. The brothers were with Him in the garden when Jesus prayed for His Father to let the cup pass.

Even though Jesus had warned the disciples that His death was imminent, they were in denial. They expected Jesus to establish an earthly kingdom through a dramatic takeover. Instead, Jesus advanced His heavenly kingdom through His gut-wrenching sacrifice on the cross.

In what ways did Jesus' death on the cross demonstrate humility?

Read Matthew 20:23-28.

How does Jesus define greatness and honor in these verses?

What is the role of a servant?

Why did Jesus take on the role of a servant here on earth instead of assuming His rights as royalty?

A BEAUTIFUL RESPONSE

Read Mark 15:37-41; 16:1.

What was Salome doing in these verses?

Jesus endured an extremely painful death. Why do you think Salome chose to stand by and watch?

In Mark 16 we learn that Salome purchased spices to anoint Jesus' body. Buying the spices was costly and anointing the body would be tedious and gruesome.

Why would Salome choose to sacrifice in this way?

When we first meet Salome, she misunderstands Jesus and what it means to be His follower, but she clearly has a change of heart after that encounter. In the final pages of her recorded story, we see a woman who embraces the power of humility.

Do you identify more with Salome in Matthew 20 or later in Mark 15 and 16? Use the prompts below as a heart check.

In my relationship with Jesus I...
    a. want to serve Him   b. want Him to meet my needs

In my relationships with others I...
    a. think of others first   b. think of myself first

If something makes me uncomfortable I...
    a. avoid it at all costs   b. am willing to do hard things

I want people to...
    a. notice me   b. feel loved by me

THINK ABOUT IT

Jesus turns Salome's understanding of Him upside down by teaching that the first shall be last. In other words, He is saying that you must be willing to serve sacrificially to be great in the kingdom of God.

Think back over this past year. Can you think of examples where you put yourself last in order to serve others? What did you learn about humility?

How about moments when you thought of your own needs ahead of others? What were the results?

✣ DAY 1: RETHINKING GREAT

What makes you feel important?

In His encounter with Salome, Jesus challenged our human perspective of greatness. Don't miss the main point of the lesson He taught her and the disciples.

According to Matthew 20:26, the secret to being great is to be a _____.

What does it mean to be someone's servant?

A great way to define servant is to pull out the root word, *serve*. A servant is simply someone who serves others.

According to Matthew 20:27, the secret to being first is to be a _____.

What does it mean to be a slave?

Jesus isn't talking about becoming a literal slave, as in someone who is owned by another human. But He does ask us to take on the mindset of a slave by putting others first. He gives us a brand new definition of greatness. It doesn't come through power, wealth, or accomplishments—it comes through serving others.

Most halls of fame celebrate those who are great because they've put themselves first. If Jesus were to create a hall of fame, it would celebrate those who served selflessly. Think of the people in your own life. Who do you know that would make the hall of fame by Jesus' standards? Write their names below.

✣ DAY 2: LEARNING CURVE

Review Matthew 20:20-21.

How would you describe Salome's understanding of Jesus in this encounter?

Review Mark 15:40-41 and Mark 16:1.

How would you describe Salome's understanding of Jesus in this encounter?

As we study Salome's story, we see a clear pattern of growth. When we first saw her, she had some obvious misunderstandings about Jesus. The last time we read about her in Scripture, she was totally devoted to Him. Her story reminds us that following Christ is a daily process of growth.

Draw a line below that illustrates your relationship with Christ. Is it a zig zag, full of ups and downs? Do you go forward in your learning about Him and then occasionally take a few steps back? Have you grown in a slow and steady upward slope?

Very few of us can look at our walk with Christ as a straight line. God graciously teaches us more about Himself and helps us to become more like Him. Salome's story helps us see faith in Christ as a process. It encourages us to continue walking with Him, learning about Him, and loving Him more with every encounter.

✢ DAY 3: UPSIDE DOWN

Jesus took what Salome and the disciples thought they knew about greatness and turned it upside down. He gave them an entirely new perspective. We often find Jesus challenging conventional wisdom through His teachings.

Take a look at these examples of other scenarios where Jesus offered a brand new perspective. Look up each verse and fill in what Jesus said.

Conventional wisdom says: Love your neighbor but hate your enemy.
 ✢ **In Matthew 5:43-44, Jesus says...**

Conventional wisdom says: If someone hurts you repeatedly, stop forgiving them.
 ✢ **In Matthew 18:21-22, Jesus says...**

Conventional wisdom says: Make sure you've got clothes to wear and food to eat.
 ✢ **In Luke 12:27-29, Jesus says...**

Can you think of a time when Jesus turned your thinking upside down and offered you a brand new perspective?

✥ DAY 4: JESUS AND YOU

What would you change in your school, family, and world if you were in charge?

✥ School:

✥ Family:

✥ World:

The reality is that you are not in charge. Understanding who is really on the throne is a huge step toward humility.

Read Revelation 4 then draw a picture of the scene described in this passage below.

Think about the 24 elders described in this passage. These are individuals with power and authority. They are dressed in fine clothes and each have a crown on their heads as a signal of royalty, yet what does this passage describe them doing over and over? (vs. 10)

Even though others would look at these elders and see greatness, they assume a position of lowliness by falling down before Jesus and casting their crowns at His feet. This is a demonstration of humility. Humility is not the byproduct of thinking poorly of yourself. Instead it is understanding your true position before a holy God. Jesus is the One who sits on the throne in the throne room of heaven. He is the only One worthy to rule, yet He demonstrates humility.

With that in mind, cast your crown before the King of kings. In the crown, write down those things that the world says makes you great or important. Surrender them to the Servant King. Ask Jesus to show you how to live more like Him by serving others.

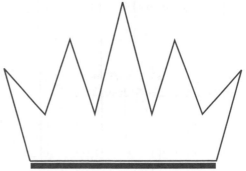

SESSION 8
JESUS LIVES:
The Encounter that Changes Everything

What do these moments have in common?

- ❖ Dorothy dumps water on the Wicked Witch of the West in The Wizard of Oz (Warner Bros., 1939).
- ❖ Cinderella tries on a glass slipper in front of her wicked stepmother and it fits (Cinderella, Disney, 1950).
- ❖ The tributes are alerted to a rule-change allowing two victors in The Hunger Games (Lionsgate, 2012).

Each scene represents a turning point, a game-changing moment that shifts the outcome of the story. From the death of the evil villain, to a shoe that changes a girl's future, there's something about a game-changing moment that makes us all want to stand up and cheer.

What's your favorite movie?

What was the point in the story that changed the trajectory of the plot? What was the turning point for the characters?

What have been the game-changing moments in your life? (In other words, what were the moments that changed everything?)

Mary Magdalene knew about game-changing moments. Her first encounter with Jesus marked a dramatic turning point in her life. So much so that she became among His most devoted followers. After His death, Mary had another dramatic encounter with the Savior. It was a moment that would change everything for her but it was also a moment that sent shock waves through time. It was an encounter that remains a game-changer for all of mankind, including you.

TURNING POINT: MARY MAGDALENE'S STORY
Read Luke 8:1-2.

What do we know about Mary's life before she encountered Jesus from verse 2?

What do we see about Mary's life after she encountered Jesus from this passage?

We don't know how long Mary had been oppressed by demons or much about her life before she met Jesus. But we do know that Mary's life was completely transformed by His power and grace. Meeting Jesus changed everything for Mary.

Do you tend to dwell more on your life before Christ or focus more on what life is like since meeting Him?

Make a list of ways Jesus has changed your life.

Read John 19:1-42.

Write down everything Jesus endured over the course of that day.

Review John 19:25.

Where was Mary Magdalene during Jesus' crucifixion?

I saw it all. I walked with Him as they made Him carry that heavy cross up the long hill. The crowds wouldn't stop yelling, "Crucify Him." Why couldn't they see that they were crucifying hope? They were crucifying love. They were crucifying our Savior!

I saw the soldiers fight over His clothes. I stood close enough to the cross to see the nails in His hands and feet. Even from the cross, He was thinking of others. I could barely stand to watch Him suffer, but I would not let myself be peeled away. He had given everything for me. I would stand by Him. As they removed His lifeless body, I couldn't stop asking questions. Why had this happened? How could He have died? What happened to the powerful Jesus I knew who could drive out demons, raise the dead, and heal the sick? Watching Him die was devastating.

Blessings, Mary Magdalene

What emotions do you think Mary wrestled with as she watched Jesus die?

Have you ever questioned God?

Read John 20:1-14.

What sticks out to you about this encounter?

Why do you think Mary was so upset to find the tomb empty?

Read John 20:15-16.

Why do you think Mary didn't recognize Jesus at first?

This moment was a game-changer. In fact, it changed everything. Jesus was dead. His body was in a tomb that was sealed with a stone. Mary's friend, Savior, and hope was buried. Everything seemed dark. But then…everything changed in an instant. He wasn't in the grave. The grave was empty. He wasn't dead. He was alive. Hope wasn't buried…it was resurrected.

A BEAUTIFUL RESPONSE
What would you have done first if you had been in Mary's place that day?

Who would you want to tell if you had seen the risen Jesus in person?

Read John 20:17-18.

Why do you think Jesus asked Mary not to cling to Him?

Mary might have wanted to stay in that moment forever. She may have hoped she and Jesus could remain in the garden and not have to face the angry world around them. She may have hoped if she held on tightly enough, Jesus would never be separated from her again. But Jesus made it clear that they could not simply stay there. He gave Mary a very specific mission—go and tell.

Have you ever felt God prompting you to tell others something about Him?

THINK ABOUT IT

Consider the following facts:

- ❖ Buddha's body was cremated and placed into relics.
- ❖ Muhammad is buried in a mosque in Saudi Arabia.
- ❖ The founder of Scientology was cremated and his ashes scattered in the ocean.
- ❖ The central figure of Rastafarianism is interred in a cathedral in Ethopia.
- ❖ In contrast, tourists who visit the tomb of Jesus will find that it is empty.

How would history be different if Jesus had not risen from the dead?

The fact that Jesus alone conquered death and rose from the grave is the most dramatic difference between Christianity and every other religion. The resurrection not only confirms His divinity, it reveals Jesus as our sure hope for eternity.

Since He overcame death, there is nothing in our lives or in our world that Jesus cannot overcome.

Is there anything in your life that feels impossible for Jesus to overcome?

How does the resurrection help you see that situation or problem differently?

✤ DAY 1: DEATH TO LIFE

Your body may never have been laid in a tomb, but did you realize that the Bible says you have been dead?

Read the following verses: Romans 6:23a; Ephesians 2:1.

Scripture says "the wages of sin is death." Another word for wages is *price*. The price everyone must pay for their sin is death. Because we can't fix our own sin problem, we are spiritually dead. This reality is overwhelming. But there is hope…

Write out the words of Jesus in John 5:24.

Faith in Christ moves us from the tomb created by our sin to eternal life with Him. Yes, death is still the cost of sin, but Jesus paid that price on the cross. The empty tomb reminds us that Jesus defeated sin and death in His resurrection.

Draw a picture that illustrates these truths below.

✤ DAY 2: BIG GIRLS DO CRY

Circle the word in each pair that best describes Mary Magdalene at the tomb:

Emotional	OR	Calm
Dramatic	OR	Passive
Composed	OR	Undone
Hopeful	OR	Hopeless

John chapter 20 describes an extremely emotional Mary. She can't stop crying. She reacts strongly both to the empty tomb and to Jesus when He appears to her. She begs others to help. She is distraught, dramatic, and expressive. This is not a passive moment for Mary. We don't see her trying to hold it together or act like everything is okay.

Do you think it was okay for her to express her emotions?

Review John 20:15-17.

Jesus is not afraid of Mary's emotions and doesn't shy away from her. He is tender toward her, even in her emotional state. Jesus could have appeared to someone else but He chose Mary. He knew how she would respond even before their encounter.

Do you believe Jesus has emotions too? Remember from the story of Mary and Martha that Jesus wept. Remember from the story of the Widow of Nain that Jesus was moved by compassion. The Bible also records other emotions expressed by God...

❖ **Anger** (Deuteronomy 1:37; Exodus 32:10)
❖ **Grief** (Psalm 78:40)
❖ **Pleasure** (1 Kings 3:10)
❖ **Delight** (Zephaniah 3:17)

Look back over the list above and circle any emotions you've experienced this past week.

It's okay to show God your emotional side. His encounter with Mary Magdalene shows us that Jesus can handle our emotions and will respond with tenderness.

❖ DAY 3: GO AND TELL

If you had been the first one to encounter Jesus after He rose from the dead, how would you tell others? What methods of communication would you use today?

Review John 20:17-18.

Almost immediately after appearing to Mary Magdalene, Jesus sent her on a mission. She was to go and tell others that He had risen. His resurrection is not the end of the story. Jesus wants us to tell others He has risen because it changes everything.

Read Matthew 28:18-20.

What specific things does Jesus challenge His disciples to do?

As a disciple of Christ, this is your mission as well. In this book, you have studied the character of Christ through His encounters with 11 ordinary women. You have learned about His divinity, grace, friendship, forgiveness, power, compassion, humility, and resurrection. You know who He is and what He's done and now you've got a mission to live out.

Pray through Matthew 28:19-20 and ask God to give you strength and courage to live on mission for Him.

✥ DAY 4: JESUS AND YOU

Can you think of a moment when you remember your name being called? (starting line-up, graduation ceremony, etc.)

Is there anyone you immediately recognize simply by the way they say your name?

Review John 20:15-16.

What caused Mary Magdalene to finally recognize Jesus?

When Mary first came to the empty tomb, she was so overwhelmed with grief that she could not see Jesus for who He was... until He said her name. The intimacy of the way He said her name snapped her out of her sadness. This encounter reminds us that Jesus is an intensely personal God. He calls each of us by name. His Spirit woos us as individuals.

As this study comes to a close, use the next page to write Jesus a detailed letter about what He means to you personally. Thank Him for calling you by name and for the personal encounters you have had with Him.

Dear Jesus,

Girls,

It has been my great honor to join you in peeking into the lives of 11 ordinary women who were changed by their encounters with an extraordinary Savior.

My prayer is that you've had some of your own encounters with Jesus along the way. You see, this study was never intended to be about a bunch of women. Their stories all point to someone much more important—Jesus. As you've read about His life, I hope you've seen Him for who He truly is. His presence in these stories is what made each one so meaningful.

The women we studied share this in common: their lives became a canvas upon which Jesus painted beautiful pictures of His character. Just like those women, your life has the power to point others to the amazing Savior you serve. Whatever your circumstance, you can trust the flawless character of Christ. As your faith in Jesus deepens, your story will become more about Him and less about you.

My wish for you is that you will long to spend time in His presence. And that those moments will shape how you see Him, yourself, and the world around you!

May the story continue with you.

A fan,

Erin